THROW ME A BONE

50 HEALTHY, CANINE TASTE-TESTED
RECIPES FOR SNACKS, MEALS, AND TREATS

Cooper Gillespie

With recipes by Sally Sampson

Preface by Stacy Alldredge

Photographs by Cami Johnson

SIMON & SCHUSTER

NEW YORK • LONDON • TORONTO • SYDNEY • SINGAPORE

SIMON & SCHUSTER
Rockefeller Center
1230 Avenue of the Americas
New York, NY 10020

SIMON & SCHUSTER and colophon are registered trademarks of Simon & Schuster, Inc.

For information regarding special discounts for bulk purchases,
please contact Simon & Schuster Special Sales at 1-800-456-6798
or business@simonandschuster.com

Designed by Liney Li

Manufactured in the United States of America

1   3   5   7   9   10   8   6   4   2

Library of Congress Cataloging-in-Publication Data
Gillespie, Cooper.
Throw me a bone : 50 healthy, canine taste-tested recipes for snacks, meals, and treats /
Cooper Gillespie ; with recipes by Sally Sampson ; preface by Stacy Alldredge ;
photographs by Cami Johnson.
p.   cm.
1. Dogs—Food—Recipes.   I. Sampson, Sally, 1955–   II. Title.
SF427.4.G54   2003
636.7'0855—dc22   2003059170

ISBN 0-7432-5591-7

For Max and his humans, Julie and Saul Nirenberg,

who inspired this book,

and for Lauren, Ben, and Mark,

who inspire everything else.

S.S.

For Meadows Way Highclare Fireside

and Ch. Fireside's Reginald Tuder Smith—my birth parents—

and for Susan Orlean and John Gillespie, my humans.

C.G.

ACKNOWLEDGMENTS

This book had many cooks but they didn't spoil the broth.

In fact, we have them to thank:

Cami Johnson and her assistant, Asia Kepka,

Stacy Alldredge,

Sydny Miner, David Rosenthal, Richard Pine, Carla Glasser,

and all our canine models.

contents

THROW ME A BONE

INTRODUCTION

To be honest, I never wanted to be a writer. I was perfectly happy being who I am—a very handsome Welsh springer spaniel (if I do say so myself!) in the prime of my life, busy doing the things I like to do—scratching my ears, strategizing squirrel ambushes, and napping. But I can no longer sit by passively and ignore the situation that has plagued my species since we became humankind's best friends.

In a word (or two): Dog Food.

I am prepared to address this situation and educate you humans, and in particular the forty million of you Americans who live with one or more of my brethren. Herewith, I present to you this guide to cooking good, healthy, tasty food for your dog.

I know, I know: you don't even cook for *yourself,* so why would you want to cook for your dog? And what about all that prepackaged stuff, those kibbles and nibbles and chunks and chow that you are *sure* are just fine for Spot and Bosco? And what if you cook something that the dog doesn't *like,* or is bad for the dog, or . . . or . . . or . . .

People, please! Sit! Stay! Okay, now let's get down to business. I can tell you this much: You will enjoy learning how to cook for your best friend. Your dog will love you for it. Everyone, and everydog, will be very happy once they try the recipes I've included here. Peace will reign, bellies will be full, life will be good. I promise.

There is ample evidence that you people love us dogs (what's not to love?). In the last several years, humans have displayed an admirable new consciousness about better quality pet food: I'm sure you've noticed all those premium, all-natural commercial foods that are now available, as well as healthy treats and snacks. But we dogs talk (wait—are you surprised??) and what we talk about (besides cats, new smells, and baseball) is how our humans treat us. In the last two years (okay, I'll admit it: I'm only two, but still . . .) what I've been hearing is that more and more humans are starting to prepare home cooked meals for their animals. In some cases, it's because they love their dogs and prefer the better quality of the food they can give them (have *you* ever eaten commercial dog food? I rest my case). In other cases, it's for health reasons—someone's Collie has colitis, perhaps, or their Akita has a wheat allergy. Often, it's someone who has a dog in his or her senior years who isn't thriving on dull, dry, commercial kibble.

Some of you humans (ladies and gents, I raise my paw to you!) are cooking everything you're serving to your best (fur-bearing) friends; others are just interested in mixing up the occasional biscuit or special meal to help Rover over an I-ate-a-dead-squirrel-or-a-tennis-ball-and-I-don't-feel-so-great episode. This is where I come in. Yes, humans have opposable thumbs, the mastery of written language, the ability to operate strange and wonderful machinery, but you don't *really* know how to make us something good, healthy, and tasty. Dogs do display a ferocious gusto for whatever people are eating—licorice, aspirin, foie gras, Krispy Kremes—but we have different metabolisms and digestive systems. In addition, there are certain things that people love (chocolate, coffee, Moon Pies) that we just can't eat. And there are certain things we faint over (liver, for instance) that you might not crave, but that are great for us. There are certain nutritional choices we might make (tennis ball as vegetable, for instance) that you shouldn't really encourage. In other words, humans, you need help in figuring out how to make nutritious, toothsome meals and treats for your dog and I, Cooper Gillespie, perhaps this nation's greatest dogatarian/philosopher/nutritionist/advisor/supermodel, am here to help.

Let me introduce my assistants. Sally Sampson, who has spent many years writing cookbooks for human beings (why? I'll never understand it) has taken my suggestions and devised recipes that are easy and absolutely delicious. For some reason, Sally herself does not own a dog. I do not choose to comment on that fact at this time. However, she knows her way around any recipe, and she taste-tested these on a lot of very lucky dog friends in New York and Boston. My pal Stacey Alldredge, a masterful dog trainer and nutrition consultant (she actually taught me how to sit!), analyzed all the recipes and consulted with Sally to make sure they were dog-friendly; be sure to check out her preface! The super-amazing photographs of me (okay, there are a few other dogs, too, but mine are particularly handsome) are the work of the super-amazing Cami Johnson, who knows a good-looking dog when she sees one (Ahem!). And as much as I wish I could type, I can't, so I dictated this to my human, Susan Orlean, who is an excellent typist and is even learning to be a very good dog-food cook, in spite of herself. She and my other human, John Gillespie, are so nice that I consider them honorary dogs.

Even though I would *really* rather be chasing squirrels and rolling in something that smells kind of strange, I felt I owed this book to my pals, both canine and human, at the dog run, so I've spent the last several months compiling the recipes and information here. After all, as George G. Vest put it, "The one absolutely unselfish friend that man can have in this selfish world, the one that never deserts him, the one that never proves ungrateful or treacherous, is his dog. . . . He will kiss the hand that has no food to offer; he will lick the wounds and sores that come in encounter with the roughness of the world. . . . When all other friends desert, he remains." Wow, that is *so* me. So get out your mixing spoon and your frying pan, tell your dog that dinner is on the way, and start cooking—and have fun!

Cheers,

Cooper

YOU ARE WHAT YOU EAT . . . AND SO ARE THEY!

In 1999, the American Pet Products Manufacturers Association conducted a survey and found that 84 percent of all dog owners refer to themselves as their animals' mom or dad. While this may have surprised some who read the survey, it certainly did not surprise me. More and more people are beginning to treat their pets as part of the family. From the perspective of one who has a vested interest in the well-being of your pet, I can tell you that it's about time!

I have been in love with animals all of my life. From an early age, I thought I would become a veterinarian, and spent my early years volunteering in shelters, rescuing animals, and ultimately becoming a veterinarian technician. After some schooling, however, I decided that veterinary medicine was not for me (I think it was the surgery). I realized that I could apply much of what I learned concerning behavior in humans to animals as well, and dogs in particular. I began to apprentice with master trainers and earned multiple certifications in various canine behavior therapies, as well as nutritional and holistic counseling.

For the last fifteen years, I have been a professional dog trainer and behavioral consultant. I have worked with thousands of dogs and puppies—each with his or her own set of problems and solutions—and their owners to improve both their dog's life and their bond with their pets.

I met Cooper Gillespie and his parents Susan Orlean and John Gillespie in a typical puppy consultation. We went over all the basic puppy issues of housetraining, exercise, jumping, and chewing. I asked Susan what she was feeding Cooper and she gave me the name of a well-known brand of dog food. I then asked if she supplemented Cooper's food with any "real food." "People food?" was her response, "No, of course not." I gave Susan advice on what dogs should and shouldn't eat, how much, how often, and on how to make it simple for the people who were going to cook for him and all his canine buddies. It is now three years later and Cooper—a happy, very healthy, and charming Welsh springer spaniel—primarily eats what Susan cooks for him.

Having cooked for all of my own dogs and helped many clients cook for theirs, this book has been a very exciting venture for me. Finally, here is a book with real food for our special companions, with simple and healthy recipes.

We want our dogs to have the healthiest and longest lives possible; nutrition plays an integral role in achieving optimal health. Dogs didn't always eat commercial food. Prior to World War II, Americans essentially fed the family dog whatever they were having for dinner. You don't need a Ph.D. or a degree in nutrition to feed your dog a healthy and balanced diet. The old adage "you are what you eat" is simple, yet true. Food affects how your dog behaves and feels, just as it does you. Cooking for your dog is no more complex than cooking for yourself.

There are many misconceptions about feeding your dog "real," or "human" food. One is that giving your dog real food makes your dog beg. Dogs do not beg for real food unless you feed them from your plate. If you don't want your dogs to beg, don't feed them from your plate. Give them their own chicken breast in their own bowl, and remember to have them "sit" for it.

Some people believe that real food will make your dog fat. Just like people, dogs don't get fat unless they eat too much and don't get enough exercise. Healthy, fresh meat and vegetables, when consumed in proper quantities, will not make Fido fat! And then, of course, there is the notion that feeding your dogs real food is spoiling them. Giving your dogs real food is not spoiling them; it is taking good care of them.

Food is many things to many people, and it serves many functions, not the least of which is to nourish us and our loved ones physically and spiritually. Don't we all bond over food? Don't we all celebrate with wonderful dinners? Don't we all take care of ourselves with healthy meals or splurge with a little treat?

In *Throw Me a Bone,* you will find the most dog-delicious fantasies that not even Fido could have imagined. Cooking for your dog is a win-win situation. No need to stress over presentation or taste. Your dog will appreciate every morsel, all the while thinking that you are the best chef ever!

—STACY ALLDREDGE

USERS' NOTES

Feeding recommendations for dogs vary from dog to dog, breed to breed, and honestly, human to human, depending upon many factors including activity level and metabolism. Some dogs like to eat once a day while others eat twice a day. Since we are merely good cooks and not canine nutritionists, we aren't going to tell you what to do, only a good way to do it. Your vet or behaviorist is the best source of information.

If your dog has only eaten commercial dog food or if your dog has special needs (allergies, chronic illness or condition, or pregnancy), please be sure to consult an expert.

Either way, dogs need to drink lots and lots of water, so always be sure to have fresh water available. A dog's water bowl should never ever be empty.

All the recipes in *Throw Me a Bone* are portioned for an average size dog, about 40 pounds. Whether your dog weighs twice that or half that, use common sense in adjusting recipes and portions.

We have categorized the recipes into meals, snacks, and treats. A meal is defined as a properly balanced combination of protein, carbohydrates, and fat; a snack is primarily carbohydrates and fat (lacking any or enough protein); a treat is half a snack; snacks and treats should be given in the same way you give snacks and treats to humans, and are not a substitute for a good meal.

In spite of the fact that we are suggesting you cook for your dog and use human-grade ingredients, we in no way recommend that you give your dog your own leftovers or table scraps; they will not provide your dog with the balanced diet he or she needs.

Cooking for your dog, no matter how adorable he is, is not quite the same as cooking for your family. Let's face it, a french fry that has been refrigerated is not a thrilling thing for most humans; however, it is a rare dog who will refuse it. Unless otherwise noted, all leftovers from the recipes in *Throw Me a Bone* can simply be covered, refrigerated, and enjoyed again.

STRAIGHT FROM THE PANTRY: VITAL VITTLES AND QUICK TIPS

When you don't have time to cook, but want to give your dog something fast and nutritious, any of the following foods will do in a pinch.

FOOD TO MAKE A MEAL:

Cooked instant rice

Cooked instant oatmeal

Canned chicken soup

Sliced apples with cheddar or blue cheese

Kashi or Puffins (dry cereal)

Baby carrots

Baby food

Bread

Plain yogurt (Stonyfield or other organic)

OTHER FOODS TO HAVE ON HAND:

Eggs

Noodles

Ground beef, lamb, or chicken

I never worry about diets. The only carrots that interest me are the number you get in a diamond. —MAE WEST

Meals, Light Meals, and Snacks

I F YOU PICK UP A STARVING DOG AND MAKE
HIM PROSPEROUS, HE WILL NOT BITE YOU;
THAT IS THE PRINCIPAL DIFFERENCE
BETWEEN A DOG AND A MAN.
—MARK TWAIN

pawcakes TREAT

TO MAKE A MEAL, ADD BLUEFISH CUBES (PAGE 29)

Ever hear the expression "a dog's breakfast"? I think Shakespeare or some other two-legger coined it, and I think it's meant to be insulting. Obviously Shakespeare never had anyone make him a stack of these pawcakes. If he had, he would never have suggested that we dogs don't enjoy the finest of morning meals. (Just look at my friend Ziggy who lives with Boston restaurateur Don Levy, patiently waiting for his pawcakes. In my dreams, I lap up a whole gallon of maple syrup with them but not while Susan is looking . . .) Cook only the amount you need; the excess batter can be stored in the fridge for two days.

1¾ cup unbleached all-purpose or
   whole-wheat flour

¼ cup yellow cornmeal

1 teaspoon baking soda

2 teaspoons baking powder

2 cups buttermilk

½ cup milk, skim or whole

2 large eggs

2 tablespoons vegetable oil

2 eggshells, crushed or ground

Place the flour, cornmeal, baking soda, and baking powder in a large bowl and stir to combine.

Place the buttermilk, skim milk, eggs, and oil in a small bowl and stir to combine. Add the wet ingredients and eggshells to the dry ingredients and mix until just combined. Do not overmix. Place a large nonstick skillet over medium heat and when it is hot, drop in small ladlefuls of batter. Cook until bubbles form and burst. Flip over and cook for about 2 minutes. Set aside to cool to room temperature.

YIELD: ABOUT 24 SILVER DOLLAR PAWCAKES

SERVING SIZE: 1 TO 2 PAWCAKES

> Grind or crush up eggshells and mix them into recipes to add extra calcium. Dogs have a strong need for calcium in order to counteract the high phosphorus content in meat.

MY DOG IS USUALLY PLEASED WITH WHAT I DO,
because she is not infected with the
concept of what I should be doing.
—LONZO IDOLSWINE

Grrrranola   TREAT

One fine day, Susan left her backpack open. I took a little investigative sniff, and what did I find but a bag of granola. Eureka! It was everything I love—crunchy, chewy, a little sweet, and so energy-packed that it made me feel like climbing Mt. Everest. After I had a time-out for my misbehavior, Susan asked Sally to figure out a canine version of granola, since I'd shown such enthusiasm for it. Now I get it for breakfast a few times a week, and I don't have to steal it out of her pack. This version is much better for dogs because it's got only a little bit of honey instead of the sugar that store-bought granola is loaded with. I'm crazy about it with the optional dried fruit, but that's a matter of taste.

1 cup rolled oats

½ cup pecans, chopped

¼ cup wheat germ

½ cup sunflower seeds

1 cup bran flakes

½ teaspoon vanilla extract

1 tablespoon fish oil, flaxseed oil, or olive oil

1 tablespoon honey

¼ cup dried cranberries (optional)

¼ cup dried blueberries (optional)

¼ cup grated carrots (optional)

Place a large nonstick skillet over medium-low heat. When it is hot, add the oats and pecans and cook, stirring constantly, until they just begin to turn golden, about 5 minutes. Add the wheat germ, sunflower seeds, and bran flakes, and continue cooking for another 10 minutes. Drizzle with the vanilla, oil, and honey. Mix gently. Set aside to cool. Add the berries. Cover and refrigerate up to one week. Add the carrots, if using, just prior to serving.

Flaxseed, also known as linseed, is about the same size as a sesame seed but is jam-packed with nutrition. Rich in dietary fiber and lignins, high in vitamins, minerals, and omega-3 essential fatty acids, flaxseed has been shown to slow cancer growth.

YIELD: 3 CUPS

SERVING SIZE: ABOUT ⅓ CUP

I USED TO LOOK AT [MY DOG] SMOKEY AND THINK, "IF YOU WERE A LITTLE SMARTER YOU COULD TELL ME WHAT YOU WERE THINKING," AND HE'D LOOK AT ME LIKE HE WAS SAYING, "IF YOU WERE A LITTLE SMARTER, I WOULDN'T HAVE TO."—FRED JUNGCLAUS

POPEYE'S FRITTATA MEAL

I didn't think I'd like spinach, but you know what? It's *almost* as good as lawn grass! (Just ask my friend Clover, who lives with architects Sandra and Toby Fairbank, and is a grass connoiseur.) Plus, as I learned from watching *Popeye* cartoons, it's really good for you. Baked in this puffy egg mixture, it's a perfect dish. I also like it cold—although there's almost never any left over.

Vegetable oil

4 large eggs

2 egg whites

2 eggshells, finely crushed or ground

2 garlic cloves, finely chopped

3 cups coarsely chopped fresh spinach, or chopped, cooked broccoli, asparagus, cauliflower, or mushrooms, alone or in combination

1 cup low-fat yogurt

2 cups cubed dry bread, cubed cooked potatoes, cooked rice, or cooked pasta

1 cup cottage cheese or grated cheddar cheese (optional)

Preheat the oven to 350 degrees. Lightly grease a 10-inch pie plate, 8-inch ovenproof, nonstick skillet, or 8-inch springform pan

Lightly beat the eggs and egg whites in a large bowl. Add the eggshells, garlic, spinach, yogurt, bread, and cheese, if using. Mix to combine.

Pour the mixture into the greased pan and place in the oven. Bake until slightly firm, about 35 minutes. Set aside to cool to room temperature, and cut into 4 quarters. Cover and refrigerate any extra up to 2 days.

YIELD: ONE 8- TO 10-INCH FRITTATA

SERVING SIZE: ¼ FRITTATA

> Eggs are considered the perfect protein; they are a great food for dogs, particularly those with skin problems. They also contain high levels of calcium (particularly in the yolk and shell), vitamin A, biotin, essential fatty acids, and zinc.

EGGS are very much like small boys. If you overheat them, or overbeat them, they will turn on you, and no amount of future love will right the wrong.—Anonymous

IF you eliminate smoking and gambling, you will be amazed to find that almost all an Englishman's pleasures can be, and mostly are, shared by his dog.—George Bernard Shaw

CRACKED EGG OMELET   MEAL

I *love* eggs. I'll eat them in any form (I can even have them raw, since dogs are immune to salmonella—sorry to make you Caesar salad-loving humans jealous) but what I like the most are omelets. The great thing is that Susan can make me an omelet at the same time she's making one for herself. In fact, we're a perfect pair: she likes to eat mostly the egg whites (watching calories, I guess) so she gives me the extra yolks. The vet says it's fine for me to have them (makes my coat gorgeous) unless I'm getting a little plump. No salt or pepper in mine, but feel free to go overboard with the cheese.

3 to 4 eggs, or 2 eggs plus 2 to 4 egg
   yolks

2 teaspoons canola oil

2 garlic cloves, finely chopped

2 eggshells, crushed (optional)

FILLING

¼ cup Virginia ham, chopped

¼ cup cheddar cheese, grated

¼ cup chopped, cooked mushrooms,
   roasted vegetables, potatoes,
   broccoli, or asparagus

2 tablespoons fresh blueberries

Place a medium (9- to 10-inch) nonstick omelet pan or skillet over medium heat. Beat the eggs well in a medium bowl. When the pan is hot, add the oil, making sure to cover the entire surface of the pan.

Add the eggs and garlic. When the eggs begin to set, gently shake the pan back and forth so they completely cover the bottom of the pan. Swirl the eggs until they begin to thicken. Sprinkle the filling on one half of the eggs and fold the other half over it, making a half-moon shape. Set aside to cool to room temperature. Cut into fifths. Cover and refrigerate any extra up to 2 days.

YIELD: ONE 9- TO 10-INCH OMELET, FOLDED

SERVING SIZE: ⅕ OMELET

LIFE EXPECTANCY WOULD GROW BY LEAPS AND BOUNDS IF GREEN VEGETABLES SMELLED AS GOOD AS BACON. —DOUG LARSON

THE TRUE ESSENTIALS OF A FEAST ARE ONLY FUN AND FEED. —OLIVER WENDELL HOLMES, SR.

CHICKEN SOUP WITH RICE *MEAL*

I remember the first time I smelled chicken soup: it was a dog's age ago, when I was just a puppy. I was moping around, totally bored with my bowl of dry food, when the aroma of the soup floated through the apartment. I thought I had died and gone to heaven. From that point on, anytime Susan would take out her stockpot, I would sit by the stove and whimper. I sounded pathetic. Since I'm a spaniel, I have the talent for looking incredibly sad, so I would whimper pathetically *and* look incredibly sad until finally Susan agreed to let me have my own little bowl. Then she learned that soup is actually great food for dogs—either on its own, or spooned over some dry kibble. It's also a nice meal when I have a bellyache.

3 carrots, cut in small dice

2 celery stalks, halved lengthwise and sliced

6 cups low-sodium chicken broth (or more for a soupier soup)

1 teaspoon dried thyme

2 cups cooked white rice (page 39) or brown rice (page 40), or 2 cooked medium white or sweet potatoes, cut in small dice

2 to 3 cups shredded or diced cooked chicken or turkey

Place the carrots, celery, chicken broth, and thyme in a large pot and bring to a boil over medium high heat. Reduce the heat to low and cook, partially covered, for 1 hour.

Add the rice and chicken and cook until just heated through, about 5 minutes. Set aside to cool to room temperature or if you are desperate, cool down with a few ice cubes. Cover and refrigerate any extra, or freeze in meal-size portions (thaw before using).

YIELD: ABOUT 8 TO 10 CUPS, ABOUT 5 TO 7 SERVINGS

SERVING SIZE: 1½ CUPS

Although the old wives' tale says that eating celery burns up more calories than the celery itself adds, the real benefit is in celery's phthalides, a nutrient that lowers lipids and wards off heart disease. In addition, celery contains calcium, potassium, phosphorus, sodium, and iron.

Mailman's Alphabet Minestrone   MEAL

I'm not saying I really want to bite a mailman. I'm just saying that there is something very appetizing about my postal service employee. (I mean that as a compliment, of course.) I'm also fond of the UPS guy, and very attracted to the FedEx fellow. Oh, but I digress. In order to keep my mind off the daily mail drop, Sally offered to cook up this dog-friendly minestrone that's full of letters. I like it just as it is, or mixed with kibble.

This recipe is also fine for humans (you might want to add some chopped scallions for garnish since there are no onions in the soup). This soup can be frozen to put in small containers for future use. Simply heat until thawed.

If your dog has issues with acidic foods, either skip this one or eliminate the tomatoes.

4 carrots, halved lengthwise and sliced

2 celery stalks, halved lengthwise and sliced

3 to 4 garlic cloves, chopped

2 teaspoons dried basil or oregano

1 (16 ounce) can diced tomatoes, including liquid (I like Muir Glen)

10 cups low-sodium chicken, beef, or vegetable stock, or water

½ bunch kale (4 to 5 cups, chopped)

⅓ cup alphabet pasta, rice or orzo

1 (19-ounce) can white cannelini or black turtle beans, drained and rinsed

Place the carrots, celery, garlic, basil, tomatoes, and chicken stock in a large stockpot and cook over medium heat until the vegetables are fully softened, about 1 hour. Add the kale, pasta, and beans and cook for 20 minutes more. Set aside to cool to room temperature. Cover and refrigerate up to 3 days or freeze in meal-size portions. Thaw before serving.

YIELDS: 12 TO 14 CUPS, 6 OR 7 SERVINGS

SERVING SIZE: 2 CUPS

In the hands of an able cook, fish can become an inexhaustible source of perpetual delight.

—Jean-Anthelme Brillat-Savarin

JAY'S FRESHLY CAUGHT BLUEFISH CUBES SNACK

TO MAKE A MEAL, SERVE WITH PAWCAKES (PAGE 13)

By and large we dogs have been forced to accept cats in our everyday lives. But one thing that bugs me is that the felines seem to have cornered the market on fish. This I do not understand, since we dogs love seafood (and unlike those fussy kitties, we're even willing to go swimming for it).

Sally's handsome friend John Verderese was recently regaling a crowd with fishing stories from his boyhood days on Long Island. He mentioned that when the freshly caught fish were brought home and cleaned and filleted in the backyard, Jay, his Black Lab, would patiently sit by, waiting to be tossed some morsels of raw fish. This "sushi dog's" favorite was bluefish, particularly the darker meat—which worked out nicely, because, its nutritional value not withstanding, many fickle-palated people don't like dark-flesh fish because of its oily consistency

29

and, well, fishy taste. John went on to say that ground meal from fish such as the Bunker (a close relative of the bluefish) used to be a staple ingredient of dry dog foods, but as humans have increasingly acquired a taste for fish, this tasty flavoring has all but disappeared from the canine menu. By the way, that fish oil is great for my shiny coat! (Take a look at this picture of my friend Chester, waiting for fish at East Coast Grill, owned by his human, Chris Schlesinger.)

1 cup cooked brown rice (see page 40)

½ pound skinned and boned raw bluefish, tuna, salmon, or red snapper, the darker the meat the better

4 ounce Velveeta or other soft cheese; use "light" cheese if you're watching your figure

Place all the ingredients in the bowl of a food processor fitted with a steel blade, and process until the mixture forms a paste.

Fill an ice cube tray with the mixture and put into the freezer. To serve, pop a cube from the tray (microwave it slightly) and mix with dry dog food and warm water. The warm water will quickly break up the cube and mix it in. Yum!

YIELD: ABOUT 2 CUPS, ABOUT 16 CUBES

SERVING SIZE: 2 CUBES FOR A SNACK; 3 CUBES WITH PAWCAKES FOR A MEAL

You can say any FOOLISH THING TO a DOG, and THE DOG WILL GIVE YOU a LOOK THAT SAYS, "MY GOD, YOU're rIGHT! I never WOULD'VE THOUGHT OF THAT!"—Dave Barry

The greatest pleasure of a dog is that you may make a fool of yourself with him, and not only will he not scold you, but he will make a fool of himself, too.—samuel butler

POODLE FRIES SNACK

Chloe is the first Poodle I ever met. Although she lives in New Jersey with her young human, Jack Nirenberg, she comes into New York City now and again, and we hang out in Riverside Park. Like a lot of French citizens, she is a tennis fanatic—or at least a tennis *ball* fanatic—and she loves good food. I don't mean the weird stuff like snails and pastry, but the really good dishes like the delicious potato wedges that Chloe calls *les frites*. (Remember, she's a poodle.) The dog version is roasted, not fried; after all, we don't like to get grease on our muzzles.

Of course you can use this same cooking technique for carrots or any other hard vegetable.

2 to 4 skin-on new or 2 sweet
potatoes, cut in eighths

2 tablespoons vegetable or olive oil

4 garlic cloves, finely chopped

1 tablespoon chopped fresh Italian
flat-leaf parsley leaves

Preheat the oven to 400 degrees.

Place the potatoes, oil, and garlic on a baking sheet and toss to combine. Place the sheet in the oven and bake until golden brown and tender, 35 to 40 minutes. Add the parsley, mix well, and set aside to cool to room temperature.

YIELD: 2–3 CUPS

SERVING SIZE: ABOUT ¼ CUP

CLASSIC DOGHOUSE CHOP FOR TWO   MEAL

Meat! Meat! You know how much I love meat. Did I mention I love meat? Oh, and in case you were wondering . . . I do love meat. If you're having company, this is the sort of dish that impresses. By the way, did I happen to tell you that I like meat?

Make one for you (but you'll probably want salt and pepper) and one for me.

2 filets mignons, pork chops, veal chops, or lamb chops, or 1 sirloin, T-bone, porterhouse, or rib steak (about 1½ to 2 inches thick, totaling about 1 pound)

Steamed broccoli or spinach, about ¼ cup per serving

Preheat the broiler or prepare the grill.

Place the meat about 3 to 4 inches from the heat source and cook for 3 to 4 minutes on each side, until medium rare.

TO SERVE, REMOVE THE BONE. CUT INTO ½-INCH CUBES AND MIX WITH THE BROCCOLI. COVER AND REFRIGERATE UP TO 3 DAYS.

SERVING SIZE: 1 CHOP

VEGETABLES ARE INTERESTING BUT LACK A SENSE OF PURPOSE WHEN UNACCOMPANIED BY A GOOD CUT OF MEAT.—FRAN LEBOWITZ

peanut NOODLes WITH Broccoli MEAL

I've never been to a ballgame, but I still love peanuts. In fact, I've been crazy for them since I was a pup. People often scatter peanuts around Riverside Park—for the squirrels, I guess—and when I was little, I would sneak them when no one was looking, especially the squirrels. The peanuts were so good I ate them in one gulp, including the shells. Now that I'm a sophisticated adult, I prefer them out of the shell and whipped into something scrumptious. Sally came up with this dish, which combines protein (peanuts), carbohydrates (noodles), and healthy broccoli for my vitamins.

This dish is basically Asian spicy sesame noodles without the salt or spices. Add raw baby carrots for some nice crunch and color!

1 pound rotini, shells, or tubetti

1 small head broccoli, woody end discarded, florets separated, stem peeled and julienned

FOR THE PEANUT DRESSING:

3 garlic cloves, sliced

1 large egg, room temperature (add shell, if desired)

¾ cup natural peanut butter (no salt, no sugar, no preservatives)

1 cup warm water

¼ cup canola oil

Bring 4 quarts of water to boil in a large pot. Add the pasta and cook until completely tender, about 12 minutes.

While the pasta is cooking, make the peanut dressing: place the garlic in a blender or in a food processor fitted with a steel blade; process until the garlic is chopped. Add the egg, peanut butter, and water, and process until combined. Gradually add the oil. Place the broccoli in a large bowl. Place a colander over the bowl. Pour the pasta into the colander; the hot water will blanch the broccoli. Let the

> In a recent study of ten everyday vegetables, broccoli emerged as the winner. High in fiber, calcium, vitamin C, and beta-carotene, it contains phytochemicals that prevent carcinogens from forming and getting to target cells.

36

broccoli sit until it turns bright green, about 2 to 3 minutes. Pour the broccoli into the colander with the pasta; immediately rinse both with cold water. Drain well. Dry the bowl and transfer the pasta and broccoli to it.

Pour the dressing over the cooled pasta. Mix well. Cover and refrigerate up to overnight.

YIELD: 7 TO 8 CUPS

SERVING SIZE: ABOUT 2 CUPS

I DO NOT LIKE BROCCOLI. AND I HAVEN'T LIKED IT SINCE I WAS A LITTLE KID AND MY MOTHER MADE ME EAT IT. AND I'M PRESIDENT OF THE UNITED STATES AND I'M NOT GOING TO EAT ANY MORE BROCCOLI.—GEORGE H. W. BUSH

PONGO'S PATIO PATTIES MEAL

These burgers are named for the world's most famous polka-dotted dog: Pongo, the leader of the Disney Dalmatian pack. That's because the rice gives the patties a nice speckled look. You can make this with any of your favorite ground meats—lamb, veal, or beef. Make a big batch and invite 101 of your friends.

This is a great recipe to make in advance.

1 tablespoon vegetable or olive oil
½ pound ground turkey, beef, lamb, or veal
1 cup cooked and cooled brown or white rice
½ cup low-sodium chicken or beef broth

Place a large skillet over medium-high heat and when it is hot, add the oil. Add the meat and cook, stirring, until it loses its rawness, about 5 minutes. Remove from heat; add the rice and broth, and form into silver dollar-size patties. Serve immediately. Cover and refrigerate any extra, or freeze.

YIELD: ABOUT 16 PATTIES

SERVING SIZE: 3 TO 4 PATTIES

1 cup long-grain white rice
2 cups water or chicken stock

Simple Steamed White Rice
Place the rice and water in a medium size pot and bring to a boil. Reduce heat to very low, cover, and let cook until all the liquid has been absorbed, about 15 minutes.

YIELD: ABOUT 3 CUPS

1 cup long-grain brown rice
2½ cups water or chicken stock

Simple Steamed Brown Rice
Place the rice and water in a medium size pot and bring to a boil. Reduce heat to very low, cover, and let cook until all the liquid has been absorbed, about 45 minutes.

YIELD: ABOUT 3 CUPS

For short-grain brown rice, use 2 cups of water

YIELD: 2 TO 2½ CUPS

For sushi rice, use 2 cups water and 1½ cups rice, place the rice and water in a medium-size pot and bring to a boil. Reduce heat to very low, cover, and cook until liquid is absorbed, about 15 minutes. Let stand, covered, 10 minutes.

One reason THE DOG HAS SO MANY FRIENDS:
HE WAGS HIS TAIL INSTEAD OF HIS TONGUE.
—UNKNOWN

SUSHI `TREAT`

Before I tell you about dog sushi, let me tell you a little about myself. Susan christened me Cooper because one of her father's best friends was named Elmer Cooper, and she always was fond of the name. Another reason was that she had never met another dog named Cooper and she thought it would be nice to have a uniquely named dog rather than the average Joe or Rover. And of course it's a handsome name, and I'm a handsome fellow. Anyway, one day I was out walking (with Susan) and we encountered the most remarkable creature: a pint-sized red sled dog with a curlicue tail, who looked exactly like one of those Iditarod musclemen, only in miniature. Amazing! I tried talking to him, but I couldn't understand a single bark or growl that came out of him. After a minute or so, I heard his human say, "Okay, let's go, Cooper!" What nerve, I thought to myself, I don't even know you!

He repeated the order, and I got a little peeved—and then realized he was talking to the little mini-Malumute. Could it be there was *another* Cooper? I could tell that Susan was just as shocked as I was. She discussed this situation with the other human, who insisted that *his* Cooper was the original and *I* was the Cooper-come-lately. I peed on his foot, just to make it clear that I disagreed. Before storming off, the human mentioned that the mini-dog was a Japanese breed called a Shiba Inu, descended from some sort of imperial bloodline that I should find impressive. My final remark to him was if this squirt was an Asian prince, what was he doing with a fine Anglican moniker like Cooper, rather than something more fitting like "Noriko" or "Issey"?

Okay, there's a reason I'm telling you this story. In the months that followed this upsetting encounter with the faux-Cooper, he and I actually became friends. I nicknamed him Tobiko and we got along just fine. The nicest part is that he introduced me to all sorts of cool Japanese foods, my favorite of which is this vegetable sushi. It's so good that it made the trauma of meeting another Cooper worthwhile.

1 sheet nori (available in Asian and specialty markets), cut in half

1 cup cooked and cooled sushi rice (page 40)

½ teaspoon lightly toasted sesame seeds

1 red bell pepper or 1 carrot, thinly julienned

Soak a sushi mat in hot water for 20 minutes. Have a small bowl of cold water available.

Place one half of the nori on the sushi mat, shiny side down. The nori should be placed so that it is has more width than depth. Place ½ cup loosely packed rice on the bottom half of the nori and press it down with your fingers. (It is often necessary to wet your fingers so that the rice doesn't stick.) Sprinkle the rice with the sesame seeds and then place the vegetables in the center.

Roll the bottom of the sushi mat up, surrounding the filling with the mat as you tighten the roll. Lightly moisten the top edge of the nori. Tighten the roll by placing it in the center of the mat, and using all of your fingers to press in along the whole roll.

Repeat with the remaining nori. Cut each roll into 8 pieces with a very sharp knife. Serve immediately or cover and refrigerate no more than 4 hours.

YIELD: 16 PIECES

SERVING SIZE: 2 TO 3 PIECES

MAX'S HUNGARIAN GOULASH MEAL

My cousin Max doesn't look Hungarian—in fact, he's a Wheaten Terrier and looks more Scottish than Magyar. (Just check out his picture.) But his human, Julie, is a purebred from Budapest, and she's introduced Max to the marvels of goulash. This recipe is so good that people can enjoy it, too—just add a little salt and more spice than you put in the dog version.

Sometimes I like to add a little rice to this dish; but then it's less authentic, so Max doesn't approve.

1 teaspoon canola oil

1½ pounds beef stew meat, cut in 1 inch cubes

4 garlic cloves, thinly sliced

6 carrots, chopped

1 celery stalk, chopped

1 tablespoon Hungarian sweet paprika

4 to 5 cups low-sodium beef stock

Rice (optional)

Place the oil in a large skillet over medium heat and when it is hot, add the beef. Cook until browned on all sides. Add the garlic, carrots, celery, paprika, and stock, cover, reduce the heat to low, and cook until the meat is tender, about 1 to 2 hours. Set aside to cool to room temperature. Serve alone or with rice. Cover and refrigerate extra, or freeze in meal-size portions.

YIELD: ABOUT 5–6 CUPS

SERVING SIZE: ½ CUP PLUS ¼ CUP RICE

> Paprika, a bright red powder, is a spice that comes from a mild red pepper in the *Capsicum annum* family. While it is most often used as a garnish, paprika has a lot of flavor.

Dogs are not our whole life,

but they make our lives whole.

—Roger Caras

BOW WOW *OH WOW!* surprize cheezburgers   MEAL

Besides our freckles, our waggly tails, and our long floppy ears, my friend Jessie and I have something very important in common: we are cheese fanatics. I'm partial to Velveeta; Jessie is a cheddarhead. We do agree that this recipe for burgers is terrific. The center is canine caviar—cheese, of course!—and it gets nice and melty and gooey. Oops, I'm drooling . . .

6 ounces ground beef or turkey

1 large egg yolk

1 egg shell, ground (optional)

¼ to ½ cup cooked rice or leftover cooked oatmeal

2 tablespoon grated cheddar or Swiss cheese

Place the beef, egg yolk and shell, if using, and rice in a small bowl and mix well. Using a knife or your hands, divide the mixture into 6 equal parts, about 1½ ounces each. Flatten each part into a patty. Place ⅓ of the cheese on each of 3 patties, and place the other 3 patties on top of the cheese. Using your hands, pinch the sides together to reseal them. (The burgers can be covered and refrigerated up to one day at this point.)

To cook:
Preheat the broiler. Place the cheezburger on a broiler pan or baking sheet about 2½ to 3 inches from the heat and broil until no longer pink, about 5 to 7 minutes per side.

or
Place a cast iron skillet over high heat and heat until it is so hot that droplets of water bounce off. Add the cheezburger. Cook until no longer pink, about 5 to 7 minutes per side.

or
Prepare a grill. Place the cheezburger on the grill and cook until no longer pink, about 5 to 7 minutes per side.

Store any extra in the refrigerator, covered.

YIELD: 3 BURGERS

SERVING SIZE: 1 BURGER

Some days you're the dog, and some days you're the hydrant.—unknown

Gnashed Sweet Potatoes TREAT

OR SNACK

I recently met a Basenji (those cat-like dogs with curled tails and almond-shaped eyes who actually clean themselves like a tabby, and don't bark at all). His name is Zero and he's amazing: he wrestles like Hulk Hogan; runs like the Acela Express; and speaks with a lovely Egyptian accent. He told me that Basenjis love yams and even eat them raw. He claims it keeps their fur orange. I'm a redhead, too, so I thought I'd better investigate this. I tried some sweet potatoes raw, but I prefer this boiled-and-smashed version, which includes a little bit of molasses. I love the sweetness; Sally tells me molasses also has lots of very healthy vitamins and iron and minerals.

2 to 3 sweet potatoes, cut into large dice

1 tablespoon blackstrap molasses

2 tablespoons peanut butter (optional)

Place the potatoes in a large saucepan, cover with cold water, and bring to a boil over high heat. Boil until the sweet potatoes are tender, about 20 minutes. Drain well, transfer to a large bowl, add the molasses and peanut butter, if using, and using a fork or a potato masher, mash until smooth. Set aside to cool to room temperature. Divide into ¼ cup size patties. Serve immediately or cover and refrigerate.

YIELD: ABOUT 12 TO 16 PATTIES

SERVING SIZE: 4 PATTIES

Considered to be the world's healthiest vegetable, sweet potatoes are basically fat-free, cholesterol-free and very low in sodium. They contain even more dietary fiber than oatmeal and help promote a healthy digestive tract. One cup cooked (skin-on) provides 30 milligrams of beta-carotene, the same available in 23 cups of broccoli! They are a good source of vitamin E, vitamin B_6, potassium and iron.

Ever consider what dogs must think of us? I mean, here we come back from a grocery store with the most amazing haul—chicken, pork, half a cow. They must think we're the greatest hunters on earth!—Anne Tyler

THAT'S ALL FOLKS! P-P-PORK BURGERS MEAL

Some dogs don't like pork, but lots of my friends can hardly wait for this Greek-inspired pork dish, a savory mix of meat and spices. The spices aren't just for flavor: check the sidebar for information on what health benefits they have.

1½ to 1¾ pounds ground pork

1½ teaspoons dried Greek oregano

1½ teaspoons dried thyme

2 to 3 garlic cloves, finely chopped

⅛ teaspoon ground cinnamon

1 tablespoon vegetable oil

Place all the ingredients except the oil in a mixing bowl and combine well with a fork or with your hands. Divide into 6 patties.

Place a large skillet over medium-high heat and when it is hot, add the oil. Add the patties, waiting about 30 seconds for the pan to reheat after each addition. Cook until deeply browned and cooked throughout, about 5 to 6 minutes on each side. Serve immediately, or freeze for later use.

YIELDS: 6 PATTIES

SERVING SIZE: 1 PATTY

Native to Sri Lanka and grown in Vietnam, China, Indonesia, and Central America, cinnamon imparts a slightly woody, sweet, and spicy flavor. Cinnamon aids digestion and has antimicrobial properties, which protect against and neutralize bacteria. Cinnamon, like cumin, garlic, clove, onion, nutmeg, and celery, also has both antiseptic and disinfectant properties.

I LIKE DOGS BETTER [THAN PEOPLE]. THEY GIVE YOU UNCONDITIONAL LOVE. THEY EITHER LICK YOUR FACE OR BITE YOU, BUT YOU ALWAYS KNOW WHERE THEY'RE COMING FROM. WITH PEOPLE, YOU NEVER KNOW WHICH ONES WILL BITE. THE DIFFERENCE BETWEEN DOGS AND MEN IS THAT YOU KNOW WHERE DOGS SLEEP AT NIGHT. —GREG LOUGANIS

IF DOGS COULD TALK, PERHAPS WE WOULD FIND IT AS HARD TO GET ALONG WITH THEM AS WE DO WITH PEOPLE. —KAREL CAPEK

LITTLE Lamb Burgers　⬤ MEAL

Lamb is my meat of choice. It's easy on the stomach, rarely gives us dogs allergies, and tastes like ambrosia (well, to me, anyway). These burgers are delicious alone, or broken up and mixed with more rice. They're also perfect for humans, so you might as well make a few extra for yourself while you're making mine.

1¼ pounds ground lamb

½ cup cooked white or brown rice (pages 39 and 40)

2 garlic cloves, finely chopped

1 teaspoon Dijon mustard

3 tablespoons chopped fresh mint leaves

2 tablespoons finely chopped fresh rosemary

2 tablespoons chopped fresh Italian flat-leaf parsley leaves

2 teaspoons dried Greek oregano

Place all the ingredients in a large mixing bowl and mix gently. Divide the meat into 4 balls of equal size and form into patties.

Place a large nonstick or cast iron skillet over medium heat and when it is hot, add the burgers. Cook until medium-well done, about 4 to 5 minutes on each side. Serve immediately or freeze.

YIELD: 4 PATTIES

SERVING SIZE: 1 PATTY

GOLDIE'S Meat Loaf Cupcakes MEAL

Sally's friend Susan Benett makes these for her dog, Goldie, who's pictured here. They look like chocolate cake with cream cheese icing, but taste *so* much better—plus if you add some greens, like peas or green beans, it's a perfectly balanced meat-and-potatoes meal. If you have young humans, they'll get a kick out of making these (and we dogs will get a big kick out of eating them!).

Of course you can make the meat loaf in the more traditional loaf pan and serve the mashed potatoes on the side, but why would you?

Vegetable oil

1 teaspoon olive oil

2 to 3 garlic cloves, finely chopped

1 teaspoon dried Greek oregano

2 slices white or whole-wheat bread

½ cup milk, water, or beef stock

2 tablespoons tomato ketchup or barbecue sauce

½ cup chopped fresh Italian flat-leaf parsley leaves

2 large eggs, lightly beaten

2 eggshells, finely crushed

2 pounds lean ground beef or turkey

Preheat the oven to 350 degrees. Lightly grease 12 muffin tin cups.

Place a medium skillet over medium heat and when it is hot, add the oil. Add the garlic and oregano and cook until golden, about 7 to 10 minutes. Place in a large mixing bowl and set aside to cool.

While the garlic is cooling, soak the bread in the liquid for a few minutes until moistened. Squeeze the bread, and drain off and discard any remaining liquid. Add the bread to the cooled garlic mixture.

Add the ketchup, parsley, eggs, eggshell, and ground beef, and mix *by hand,* until everything is thoroughly

FOR THE MASHED POTATOES:

2 pounds small red potatoes or
   sweet potatoes, peeled if desired,
   and quartered

1 to 2 tablespoons canola or olive oil

2 tablespoons freshly grated
   Parmesan cheese (optional)

Blueberries for garnish

incorporated. Divide into 12 equal portions and place in prepared muffin tin cups. Bake until the mixture is firm, about 45 minutes.

For the mashed potatoes:

Place the potatoes in a large saucepan, cover with cold water, and bring to a boil over high heat. Reduce the heat to medium and cook until tender, 10 to 12 minutes. Drain and place in a medium mixing bowl. Mash with a fork or potato masher, gradually incorporating the oil and cheese. Ice each muffin with a generous amount of mashed potato. Top each with a blueberry. Cover and refrigerate up to 3 days.

YIELDS: 12 MUFFINS

SERVING SIZE: 2 MUFFINS

IF YOU GET TO THINKIN' YOU'RE A PERSON OF SOME INFLUENCE, TRY ORDERIN' SOMEBODY ELSE'S DOG AROUND. —COWBOY WISDOM

No man is lonely eating spaghetti; it requires so much attention.—Christopher Morley

Catch! Meatballs and Spaghetti

I'm lucky: I'm a tomato and onion-eater, and have no trouble slurping up this sauce. But some dogs just can't take such acidic foods, so be careful with this recipe. See what your dog can handle before serving a full portion. If he or she doesn't do well with them, just serve the meatballs and the pasta (pretty wonderful all on their own!).

TOMATO SAUCE:

1 tablespoon vegetable oil

3 garlic cloves, finely chopped

2 tablespoons dried basil

1 tablespoon dried Greek oregano

1 (28-ounce) can whole tomatoes in juice (I like Muir Glen)

1 tablespoon tomato paste (I like Muir Glen here, too)

For the tomato sauce:
Place a heavy-bottomed 6 to 8 quart stockpot over medium heat and when it is hot, add the oil. Add the garlic and cook until golden, 3 to 5 minutes.

Add the remaining sauce ingredients and cook, partially covered, 1½ to 2 hours, depending upon thickness desired. Stir occasionally to break up the tomatoes and keep the sauce from burning.

MEATBALLS:

1⅓ pounds ground beef or turkey

½ cup finely chopped fresh Italian flat-leaf parsley leaves

½ cup cottage cheese

1 pound linguine

For the meatballs:

Place the meat, parsley, and cottage cheese in a medium bowl and combine well. Divide into 24 parts and form into meatballs.

In a nonstick skillet, cook the meatballs until browned on all sides. Cover with tomato sauce and cook over low heat until cooked through, about 15 minutes.

Bring a large pot of salted water to a boil. Cook the pasta until al dente, 10 to 12 minutes. Drain well.

To serve:

Mix all together and watch the show: this is very cartoon-y to watch. Cover and refrigerate up to 3 days.

YIELD: 24 MEATBALLS; ABOUT 3 CUPS SAUCE; 7 CUPS LINGUINE

SERVING SIZE: 4 MEATBALLS; ½ CUP SAUCE; ABOUT 1 CUP OF LINGUINE

I am not a GLUTTON—I am an explorer of food.

—Erma Bombeck

veggie salad

A lot of humans don't realize that dogs like vegetables. Susan started giving me baby carrots when I was a puppy; when she saw how much I liked them, she started offering me everything else in the vegetable patch. I like it all, even lettuce (I'm partial to endive, in fact). And vegetables are so good for me that I could howl. Next time you're craving something crunchy and have eaten more than your fair share of biscuits, try this veggie salad instead: it is low-calorie and nearly fat-free, so it won't slow you down when you're squirrel-chasing. To a human, this dish might look a little sloppy, but the rough texture is perfect for a dog.

1 apple, skin-on, cored and coarsely chopped

2 garlic cloves, finely chopped

2 carrots, unpeeled, coarsely chopped

1 cup Brussels sprouts, coarsely chopped

1 cup green beans, coarsely chopped

1 to 2 zucchini, shredded or coarsely chopped

1 small head cabbage, coarsely chopped

2 tablespoons apple cider vinegar

2 tablespoons honey or maple syrup (optional)

Place all the ingredients in the bowl of a food processor fitted with a steel blade. Pulse until it comes together. Serve immediately, or freeze for later use.

YIELDS: ABOUT 3 TO 3½ CUPS

SERVING SIZE: ½ CUP PER SERVING

LOOK! A BIRDY! BURGERS   SNACK

TO MAKE A MEAL, ADD GREENS

Hey! Did someone say bird? Where? Which way? Where'd it go?? Oops, sorry, I misunderstood. Oh, yes, birdy burgers—a great favorite of mine. Ground turkey is really mild, so it's great for dogs with touchy digestion. Me, I just love the taste.

1½ to 1¾ pounds ground turkey,
beef, or lamb, or a combination
3 garlic cloves, finely chopped
1 whole egg or 2 egg yolks
½ teaspoon ground cinnamon
1 cup cooked brown or white rice
(pages 39 and 40)

Place the turkey, garlic, egg, cinnamon, and rice in a bowl and mix well to combine. Divide the mixture into 6 burgers.

Place a large skillet over medium-high heat and when it is very hot, add the burgers one at a time, making sure to let the pan reheat between additions. Cook until deeply browned, about 3 to 5 minutes on each side. Serve immediately, or freeze for later use.

YIELDS: 6 BURGERS

SERVING SIZE: 1 BURGER

I named my dog stay . . . so I can say
"come here, stay. come here, stay."
—steven wright

67

POOCHIE'S PASTA PRIMAVera ⬭ MEAL

This easy dish is great for a quick dog meal-on-the-go. The sauce is made lickety-split in your food processor. If you want to add protein, throw in a hard-boiled egg or some tofu.

½ head broccoli, stem and florets chopped

2 cups spinach, baby carrots, or Brussels sprouts, or a combination

½ cup lightly toasted pine nuts

1 cup grated Parmesan cheese

2 to 3 garlic cloves, finely chopped

½ cup chopped fresh Italian flat-leaf parsley leaves

2 tablespoons olive or vegetable oil

1 tablespoon red wine vinegar

½ pound bow tie or shell pasta, cooked, drained, and slightly cooled

Place the broccoli, spinach, pine nuts, Parmesan cheese, garlic, parsley, oil, and vinegar in the bowl of a food processor fitted with a steel blade, and process until combined. Cover and refrigerate up to overnight. Pour over the pasta, stir well and serve immediately.

YIELD: 3 TO 4 CUPS

SERVING SIZE: 1 TO 1½ CUPS

> To toast pine nuts: place on baking sheet in preheated 300 degree oven. Bake for about 10 minutes, checking occasionally. Remove from sheet to cool.

> Spinach, a great source of antioxidants, contains twice the iron found in most other green vegetables.

OLD YELLER'S CHICKEN   MEAL

I named this dish for my favorite book. Remember the scene at the end . . . no, don't get me started! I cry every time I think about it. Anyway, when you talk about a dog's dream dish, you're talking about chicken. This is a great basic recipe for roasting.

1 whole roaster chicken (4 to 5 pounds) or capon (6 to 7 pounds)
1 tablespoon olive oil
1 teaspoon garlic powder

Preheat the oven to 450 degrees. Remove and discard the giblets from the chicken cavity. Rinse the chicken, including the neck, in several changes of cold water and pat dry.

Rub the chicken with the oil and sprinkle all over with the garlic powder. Place the chicken and chicken neck on a rack in a roasting pan. Bake for approximately 40 to 70 minutes (10 minutes per pound). Do not baste. If you are using a thermometer, place it deep in the inner thigh: the chicken is done when the internal temperature reaches 160 degrees. If you do not have a thermometer, you can tell when the chicken is done when the juices run yellow and clear from the breast, and the leg moves easily.

Remove and discard the bones. Remove and finely chop the skin. Cool to room temperature. Cover and refrigerate up to 5 days.

SERVING SIZE: 1 TO 1¼ CUPS

You may have a DOG THAT WON'T SIT UP, ROLL over or even COOK BREAKFAST, NOT BECAUSE SHE'S TOO STUPID TO learn HOW BUT BECAUSE SHE'S TOO smart TO BOTHER.—RICK HOROWITZ

A DOG IS NOT almost HUMAN, AND I KNOW OF NO greater INSULT TO THE canine race THAN TO DESCRIBE IT AS SUCH.—JOHN HOLMES

Terrier Tofu MEAL

Susan's first dog—not her best, of course, but her first—was a West Highland White Terrier named Duffy who was small, square, and white. Sort of like a chunk of tofu, when you think about it, which is why we named this dish in his honor. Even though I'm not a vegetarian, I love tofu; it's a great source of protein and mixes perfectly with just about anything. This dish is a great everyday meal, and you can make a big batch and serve it all week long.

I love this with steamed rice (page 39).

1 tablespoon vegetable oil

2 garlic cloves, finely chopped

1 tablespoon finely chopped fresh ginger root

1 pound firm or extra firm tofu, cut into ½ inch cubes

2 large eggs, beaten

½ cup shredded carrots

½ cup fresh bean sprouts

Place the oil in a large wok or skillet over high heat and when it is hot, add the garlic, ginger, and tofu and cook for 1 minute. Add the eggs and carrots and cook until the mixture just begins to firm up, about 1 minute. Lower the heat and cook for an additional minute, being careful not to overcook the eggs. Let cool to room temperature and garnish with the bean sprouts. Cover and refrigerate.

YIELD: ABOUT 4 CUPS

SERVING SIZE: ABOUT ¾ CUP

In order to really enjoy a dog, one doesn't merely try to train him to be semi-human. The point of it is to open oneself to the possibility of becoming partly a dog.

—EDWARD HOAGLAND

Tuna Training Treats

TREAT

My friend Rachel Friedman, a wonderful dog trainer in Cleveland, Ohio, came up with this ingenious recipe for treats. They're easy to make and last for at least two months in the freezer. They're so good that even an ornery dog will behave in order to get one! Better still, they smell so good that they'll get any dog's attention, yet won't offend those sensitive human noses.

Vegetable oil

2 (6-ounce) cans tuna in water or 1 can (14 to 15 ounces) salmon, undrained

2 large eggs

1 to 1½ cups rice flour or unbleached all-purpose flour

1 tablespoon garlic powder

Freshly grated Parmesan cheese

Preheat the oven to 350 degrees. Lightly grease an 8-inch square cake pan.

Place the tuna, including the water, in a bowl and mash with a fork until the clumps are out. Transfer to a blender or food processor fitted with a steel blade and process until liquefied. Add the eggs and extra water, a little at a time, if needed to liquefy completely. Pour into a mixing bowl, add the flour and garlic powder, and mix until it has the consistency of cake mix. Spread into the prepared pan and sprinkle with *lots* of Parmesan cheese. Bake until the edges pull away and the texture is like putty, about 15 minutes. Turn out of the pan and let cool. Using a pizza cutter, cut into teeny squares. These freeze beautifully.

YIELD: 64

SERVING SIZE: 2 TO 3 TREATS

Grrrround Turkey Turkeys TREAT

TO MAKE A MEAL, ADD GREENS OR PAWCAKE (PAGE 13)

I love chasing the wild turkeys that live near my country house. I've never caught one (and probably never will) but I can console myself with this great recipe. Don't worry if your turkeys end up looking a little freeform: they'll taste just as good in any shape.

1 pound ground turkey

2 large eggs (add ground shell if desired)

2 cups cooked white or brown rice (pages 39 and 40)

2 carrots, cut in small dice

1 apple, cored but skin-on, cut in small dice

Preheat the oven to 375 degrees. Line a baking sheet with parchment paper.

Place all the ingredients in a bowl and mix until combined. Form into 4 turkey shapes and place on the baking sheet. Bake 45 minutes. Set aside to cool. Serve immediately or freeze for later use.

YIELD: 4 "TURKEYS"

SERVING SIZE: 1 "TURKEY"

Don't accept your dog's admiration as conclusive evidence that you are wonderful.—Ann Landers

TYLER'S BURRITO MEAL

Stacy Alldredge, my beloved trainer (not that I really need training, but . . .) was making vegetable burritos for herself one day and realized she hadn't made dinner yet for her four dogs. She realized a burrito would make a perfect dog dinner. If your mutt is trying to lose weight, don't use the cheese—just bulk it up with more vegetables.

1 tablespoon olive oil

1 pound ground beef, chicken, or turkey

½ cup chopped broccoli, green beans, Brussels sprouts, or cauliflower

2 garlic cloves, finely chopped

½ cup cooked brown rice (page 40)

Five (12-inch) whole-wheat tortillas, cut in half

¼ cup grated cheddar cheese

Place a large skillet over medium heat and when it is hot, add the olive oil. Add the meat and cook, stirring, until it changes color, about 3 to 5 minutes. Add the broccoli and garlic and cook for 5 minutes. Remove from heat. Add the rice and mix well.

Divide the mixture equally among the tortilla halves and sprinkle with cheese. Roll up and place on plate. Cut into bite-size pieces. Serve immediately, or cover and refrigerate up to 2 days.

YIELD: 10 BURRITO HALVES

SERVING SIZE: 2 HALVES

I can train any dog in 5 minutes. It's training the owner that takes longer.—Barbara Woodhouse

salmon Burgers

TO MAKE A MEAL, SERVE 2 TO 3 BURGERS AND ADD GREENS OR STEAMED RICE (PAGE 39)

Salmon is one of my favorite foods. My friend Hilda and I often order it for lunch and take it home and eat it cold if we have any left over.

1¼ pounds salmon fillets, skinned, boned, and steamed, or 1 (14 to 15 ounce) can and 1 (7¾ ounce) can salmon

2 cups bread crumbs

1 large egg (plus shell, if desired)

2 beets, shredded

1 celery stalk, cut in small dice

2 tablespoons chopped fresh Italian flat-leaf parsley leaves

2 tablespoons chopped fresh dill

1 tablespoon olive oil

Place all the ingredients, except the oil, in a bowl and combine well. Cover and refrigerate until firm, at least one hour, or overnight. Shape the mixture into fish shapes or burgers.

Place a large skillet over high heat and when it is hot, add the oil. Add the burgers and cook until browned, 3 to 5 minutes on each side. Set aside to cool to room temperature.

YIELD: 4 TO 6 BURGERS

SERVING SIZE: ONE FOR A SNACK, 2 TO 3 FOR A MEAL

A DOG CAN EXPRESS MORE WITH HIS TAIL IN MINUTES THAN HIS OWNER CAN EXPRESS WITH HIS TONGUE IN HOURS.—ANONYMOUS

DOGGONE BEST PIZZA MEAL

I always beg for a piece of pizza whenever one is delivered, but it's not good for me—too much grease, salt, and spice, and I hate it when my fur smells like pepperoni. But I still love the concept of pizza, so Sally devised this dog-friendly version, which I now think is far superior to anything from Domino's.

4 English muffins, split and lightly
toasted

TOPPING:

1 cup grated mozzarella cheese

4 whole tomatoes, thinly sliced and
drained on a paper towel

1 cup cooked, chopped broccoli,
spinach, kale, or squash

1 cup cooked ground turkey

½ cup sliced raw mushrooms

1 tablespoon dried Greek oregano

¼ cup chopped fresh basil

1 tablespoon goat cheese (optional)

Preheat the oven to 300 degrees.

Place the English muffin halves on a baking sheet. Divide the cheese, tomatoes, broccoli, turkey, and mushrooms evenly among the halves. Sprinkle with the oregano and basil and dot with goat cheese, if desired. Place the English muffins in the oven and bake until the cheese is melted, about 5 minutes. Set aside to cool.

YIELD: 8 PIZZAS

SERVING SIZE: 2 PIZZAS

Gennaro Lombardi, a baker who emigrated from Naples in 1895, is credited with bringing pizza to America. When his pizza (made from the same dough recipe his father and grandfather used in Naples) sold better than his breads, he abandoned the bakery and opened the first pizzeria on Spring Street in New York City in 1905. His grandson still operates it, a few doors down, with the same oven.

Lotsa Liver and Rice   MEAL

You humans don't know what you're missing when you turn your noses up at liver. There's almost nothing more scrumptious. That smell! That taste! Well, if you don't want it, it's just as well: that means there's more for us dogs. Go easy with the portions on this, since liver's pretty rich.

1 tablespoon olive oil

2 garlic cloves, finely chopped

2 cups liver, cut in small dice or diced raw beef, pork, or chicken

2 cups cooked white or brown rice (pages 39 or 40)

1 cup assorted vegetables, such as sweet potato, carrots, white potato, cut in small dice, or chopped fresh spinach, kale, Brussels sprouts, or green beans

½ to 1 cup water

Place a large skillet over medium high heat and when it is hot, add the oil. Add the garlic and cook until golden, 3 to 5 minutes. Add the remaining ingredients and bring to a boil over medium heat. Lower the heat and cook 20 minutes. Serve immediately or freeze for later use.

SERVING SIZE: 1½ CUPS

Liver is a great source of quality protein and essential fatty acids (including both omega-3 and omega-6) and should be eaten often but not in large quantities. It contains vitamins A, C, D, E, and K, and is an first-rate source of zinc, manganese, selenium, and iron. It also contains all the B vitamins, particularly B_2, B_3, B_5, biotin, folic acid, B_{12}, choline, and inositol.

mack and cheese MEAL

TO MAKE A MEAL, ADD ONE SALMON BURGER (PAGE 82) OR DESSERT LIVER TREATS (PAGE 109)

My friend Moose and I have been searching for the perfect recipe for using the Wonderful Food Known as Cheese. Moose's human, David Strymish, owns Jessica's Biscuit, the cookbook catalog, so Moose spent a lot of time researching. This canine take on mack and cheese is divinely cheesy. It also makes the most delicious leftovers.

If your dog has a sensitive stomach, substitute tofu cheese for the Romano and mozzarella.

½ pound macaroni, shells, or tubes

1 tablespoons vegetable oil

1 tablespoons all-purpose flour

1¼ cups milk

½ cup shredded cheddar cheese

¼ cup shredded Gruyère cheese

¼ cup grated Romano cheese

½ (28-ounce) can whole tomatoes, well-drained and chopped (optional)

TOPPING

3 tablespoons grated Romano cheese

¼ cup shredded mozzarella cheese

½ cup bread crumbs

Preheat the oven to 350 degrees. Lightly grease an 8 x 8-inch baking pan. Bring a large pot of water to a boil. Add the pasta and cook until al dente, 6 to 10 minutes depending on type. Drain the pasta and set aside in a large mixing bowl.

Place the oil in a medium saucepan over medium heat and when it is hot, add the flour, stirring all the time. As soon as it colors slightly, gradually add the milk, stirring all the time. Gradually add the cheddar, Gruyère, and Romano cheeses, stirring until the cheeses are melted. Add the sauce to the pasta and stir to combine. Add the tomatoes, if using, and pour into the prepared baking pan.

Bet you didn't know that macaroni and cheese was President Ronald Reagan's favorite dinner. When he was in the White House, it was served to him on every birthday. According to *The White House Family Cookbook*, by Henry Haller and Virginia Aronson, Reagan liked his with dry mustard and Worcestershire sauce, which as you can see, I don't.

Place the topping ingredients in a small bowl, toss to combine, and sprinkle evenly over the pasta. If not baking immediately, cover with plastic wrap and refrigerate up to 2 days. Bake until golden, about 35 minutes. Serve at room temperature. Cover and refrigerate up to 5 days.

YIELD: 6

SERVING SIZE: ¾ CUP

THE BIG BIRD AND CHEESE MELT

Okay, here's something that makes me wag with pleasure: bird plus cheese. These are the two major food groups, in my opinion, and certainly a dog's best friends (besides you humans, of course). This is easy to put together for your pooch, and is a great high-protein meal—perfect for a sporty guy like me.

4 thick slices cooked turkey, dark meat, light meat, anything as long as there are no bones.

4 thin slices cheddar cheese

Preheat the broiler. Place the turkey slices on a baking sheet and top with thin slices of cheese. Place under the broiler until the cheese melts, about 1 to 2 minutes. Set aside to cool to room temperature. Cover and refrigerate up to 5 days.

YIELD: 4 MELTS

SERVING SIZE: 2 MELTS

If a dog jumps in your lap, it is because he is fond of you; but if a cat does the same thing, it is because your lap is warmer.
—ALFRED NORTH WHITEHEAD

No more turkey, but I'd like another helping of that bread he ate.
—Anonymous, quoted in *JOY OF COOKING*

Treats and Biscuits

BreatH-sweetenInG Biscuits ⬭ TREAT

I'm a big kisser. That means I have to be very careful to keep my breath as sweet as can be: no one's going to accuse *me* of having Dog Breath. Parsley or mint is the perfect way to freshen up between brushing, and these biscuits are an easy and enticing way to get a good dose.

3 cups unbleached all-purpose white or whole-wheat flour, or a combination

1 tablespoon baking powder

1 teaspoon baking soda

½ cup vegetable shortening

1 cup buttermilk or low-fat yogurt

1 tablespoon honey

¼ cup chopped fresh Italian flat-leaf parsley or mint leaves

Preheat the oven to 425 degrees. Line a baking sheet with parchment paper.

Place the flour, baking powder, and baking soda in the bowl of a food processor fitted with a steel blade and mix to combine. While the processor is going, add the shortening, a few pieces at a time, and process until the mixture resembles cornmeal. Transfer the mixture to a large bowl, add the buttermilk, and mix by hand until combined. Mix in the honey and parsley. Divide the mixture into 24 pieces, flatten them, and place them on the prepared baking sheet. Place the sheet in the oven and bake until golden brown, 12 to 15 minutes. Set aside to cool to room temperature.

YIELD: 24 BISCUITS

SERVING SIZE: 2 TO 3 BISCUITS

Parsley is thought to have originated in Sardinia. We prefer the more flavorful Italian flat-leaf parsley to the more ubiquitous curly, which while milder is also more bitter. Slightly tangy and peppery, it is known as a breath freshener. (Not that I need it! But some of my four-footed friends who eat too much garbage do.)

paw-mesan tail twisters   `TREAT`

I guess cheese is one of the themes of this book (as well it should be). Here it's baked into the world's finest wag-inspiring treat. If you make the twists very small, they're great training treats. Make them a little bigger—*please!!!*—and you've got a perfect nibble for anytime between meals.

2 cups whole-wheat flour

¼ cup yellow cornmeal

1 large egg (add shell if desired)

¾ cup skim milk or water

½ cup freshly grated Parmesan cheese

Preheat the oven to 325 degrees. Line a baking sheet with parchment paper.

Place the flour, cornmeal, egg, skim milk, and ¼ cup of the Parmesan cheese in a bowl and mix well, kneading with your hands.

Place the remaining ¼ cup of Parmesan cheese on a plate. Using your hands, tear off tablespoon-size pieces of dough and form into small logs. Roll the logs in the Parmesan cheese, then twist. Place the twists on the baking sheet. Bake for 30 minutes. Set aside to cool. Place in an airtight container and store up to 2 weeks.

YIELD: ABOUT 36 TO 48 PIECES

SERVING SIZE: 2 FOR A TREAT; 3 FOR A SNACK

LILY'S LOVELY Frozen Parfait   TREAT

Rachel Friedman, my dog-trainer friend, makes this amazing parfait and stuffs it into a big rubber Kong for her dog Lily. It's so good that Lily will sit for an hour or two, chomping on her Kong until she gets every bit of the parfait out of it. This keeps Lily from noticing that Rachel isn't home, which is good, since Lily has classic separation anxiety, and uses it as an excuse to eat shoes, woodwork, carpeting, and trash. I myself am far too well-adjusted to suffer from any such neurotic displacement; but I still do love the taste of this parfait.

AMOUNTS WILL VARY DEPENDING ON THE ARTICLE BEING STUFFED (SEE BELOW).

Peanut butter (optional)

Cream cheese (optional)

Plain yogurt

Cinnamon (optional)

Cheerios or other oat cereal, or granola

Banana, sliced thin

Chopped apple or pear

Chopped nuts, such as walnuts, almonds, shelled sunflower seeds, etc.

For added flavor you can stir in ½ teaspoon of cinnamon per cup of plain yogurt. Or just use plain.

The parfait can be made in a large Kong or a hollow bone or a biscuit ball. Be sure to plug up the small end of the Kong or hollow bone and the three smaller bone-shaped holes in a biscuit ball (small or medium) with either duct tape or a layer of peanut butter or cream cheese, which you freeze before adding the following.

Layer in Kong, biscuit ball, or hollow bone: yogurt, cereal or granola, yogurt, banana, yogurt, apple, yogurt, nuts, yogurt.

Place in freezer for at least 6 hours, or overnight. Serve and watch the fun!

Dogs feel very strongly that they should always go with you in the car, in case the need should arise for them to bark violently at nothing right in your ear. —Dave Barry

GO-Bananas Training Treats   TREAT

I personally have an issue with coming when I'm called. It's not that I don't intend to *ever* come; it's just that I'm usually in the middle of doing something really interesting when Susan calls me. As a result, I tend to dawdle, and Susan tends to get a little, uh, exasperated. Then one day, she brought one of these treats with her when we went out for a walk, and when she called me to come, she held up a treat. Suddenly it all made sense: if I showed up in a hurry when she called, I would get one. What a scam! I mean, really—just for coming to say hello, I got a delicious oatmeal nibble. (This is a great can't-miss deal, my fellow dogs: I suggest you look into it with your humans.)

Mix up a batch of these, and you can cut them into any size or shape you want: tiny squares for training a Teacup Poodle, more substantial chunks for motivating a Mastiff . . .

Vegetable shortening

3 to 4 large eggs

⅓ cup canola or corn oil

⅓ cup honey

⅓ blackstrap molasses

1 cup skim milk

3 ripe bananas, mashed

3 cups whole-wheat flour

3 to 6 cups uncooked oatmeal, depending on texture preferences

Preheat the oven to 325 degrees. Lightly grease a 10 x 15-inch baking sheet with vegetable shortening.

Place the eggs, oil, honey, molasses, milk, and mashed bananas in a bowl and mix with a hand blender. Add the flour and oatmeal and mix until it has the consistency of cake mix. Let the dogs lick the spoon and bowl!

Spread the batter in the prepared pan. Bake 1 hour; turn off the oven, and let the treats sit until the oven cools. Turn out onto the counter or a cutting

Blackstrap molasses is the thick, very dark brownish-black syrup that remains after the last extraction of sugar from cane or sorghum. Strong and slightly bitter-tart in flavor, it has the lowest sugar content of all types of molasses and is more nutritious than other sweeteners.

board and using a pizza cutter or knife, cut into whatever shapes suit your fancy (or break into pieces). Dogs don't care! Cover and refrigerate or freeze up to 2 months.

YIELD: DEPENDS ON THE SIZE YOU MAKE THEM

SERVING SIZE: 2 TO 3 PIECES

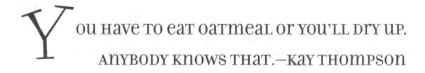

You have to eat oatmeal or you'll dry up. Anybody knows that.—Kay Thompson

sunflower cookies `TREAT`

Some dogs are cookie freaks. They faint at the sight of one. They start drooling the minute someone whispers the word. Me, I never saw the point of cookies (I'm more of a meat-head) until I tasted one of these. The flavor of the sunflower seeds just knocks me out. Now I know why those birds hang out at the feeder all the time.

2 cups whole-wheat flour

⅔ cup yellow cornmeal

½ cup shelled sunflower seeds or pumpkin seeds

2 tablespoon corn oil

½ cup beef, vegetable, or chicken broth

3 large eggs

¼ cup lowfat milk

Whole-wheat or unbleached all-purpose flour for the work surface

Preheat the oven to 350 degrees. Line a cookie sheet with parchment paper.

Place the flour, cornmeal, and seeds in a large bowl and mix to combine. Place the oil, broth, 2 of the eggs, and the milk in a small bowl, mix well. Add to dry mixture. Mix well; the dough should be firm. Let rest 15 to 20 minutes.

Lightly flour a work surface. Place the dough on the work surface and roll out to ¼ inch thick. Cut into shapes with a cookie cutter. Place the shapes on the baking sheet.

Beat the remaining egg in a small bowl, and lightly brush on the cookies. Place the baking sheet in the oven and bake until golden brown, 25 to 35 minutes. Cool. Store cookies in airtight container.

YIELD: 4 TO 5 DOZEN

SERVING SIZE: 2 TO 3 PIECES

> Low in sodium (unless they are salted, which is a no-no) and high in protein, potassium, fiber, and all the B vitamins, sunflower seeds are a great addition to cookies, cereals, burgers, and breads.

Danny's Dog Sundae TREAT

Young Danny Benett, the human who takes care of Goldie the dog, is a budding and innovative chef. Here is his recipe, word for word, for what he likes to make for Goldie.

Chicken livers, cut up into dog-sized pieces

One dog treat (store bought) grinded up

Fry the liver in a pan. Cut up into small tidbits. Put cooked liver into dog's bowl. Then sprinkle grinded dog treat on top like sprinkles. Feed to dog after dinner as dessert (but this may be too much for a dog to eat after dinner).

YIELD: 1 SUNDAE

SERVING SIZE: 1 SUNDAE

Dessert Liver Treats TREAT

TO MAKE A MEAL, ADD MACK AND CHEESE (PAGE 89)

These are pretty stinky, at least to the human nose, but are delicious and perfumey to us. Make a really big batch so you only smell up your house once (but end up with a *nice* quantity of liver goodies).

Beef liver, cut into 1-inch cubes

Preheat the oven to 325 degrees. Line a baking sheet with parchment paper.

Place the livers on the baking sheet and put in the oven. Bake until the livers are dehydrated, 45 minutes to 1 hour. Let cool. Store in an airtight container up to one month.

SERVING SIZE: 1 TO 2 PIECES

POLENTA SQUIRRELS   TREAT

There is nothing—I mean *nothing*—in this world more interesting to me than squirrels. Every morning I do two laps of the park, checking the trees for them, and rounding up any of the bushy-tailed intruders I can. They use all means—stealth, cunning, deceit, scary noises, nut-throwing—to fend me off, but I am dogged and true. I once got really close to one; I could smell the acorns on his breath and almost feel his bristly fur against my face. But then—the coward!—he launched himself into a tree and was gone in an instant. I was totally dejected. Am I a dog or a mouse? I asked myself. Am I going to be outdone by some rodent with beady eyes and an overbite? Such musings depressed me, so Susan asked Sally for a recipe that might help ease my pain. Sally came up with these amazing squirrel-shaped snacks, which I suspect taste much better than the real thing. (By the way, if you're more into bunnies or birds, feel free to tell your human to shape the polenta to your preference.)

Vegetable oil

4½ cups water

1 cup coarsely ground cornmeal

¼ cup chopped fresh Italian flat-leaf parsley leaves

¼ cup grated Parmesan cheese (optional)

Lightly oil a 9-inch pie pan or 8 x 8-inch pan.

Place the water in a medium saucepan over high heat and when it comes to a boil, gradually stir in the cornmeal. Reduce the heat to medium-low and cook until it thickens, about 20 minutes, stirring frequently. Add the parsley and the Parmesan cheese, if using. Pour in the prepared pan and refrigerate until cooled and solid, at least 20 minutes or up to 4 hours. When it has cooled completely, use a cookie cutter to cut it into shapes. Store in airtight container up to two weeks.

YIELD: APPROXIMATELY 6 SQUIRRELS

SERVING SIZE: 2 TO 3 PIECES

corn DOG BISCUITS TREAT

I tasted corn for the first time last summer after Susan had friends over for a barbecue. I decided to do a quick check of the trash before it went out (Susan and her friends were at the movies, I believe) and found the leftover cobs from grilled corn. Yes, the trash was already in a bag in the garage, and yes, it was supposed to be off-limits, but that's not my point; all I'm trying to say is that I learned that evening that corn is one of the all-time great flavors. These biscuits are as corny as can be.

1 cup yellow cornmeal

1½ cups whole-wheat or unbleached all-purpose flour

2 teaspoons baking powder

2 to 3 tablespoons honey

1 large egg, lightly beaten (plus eggshell, if desired)

1½ cups plain yogurt, preferably Stonyfield

2 tablespoons vegetable oil, plus additional for the pan

1 cup (1 small can) creamed corn (optional)

½ cup finely chopped turkey or chicken hot dogs (optional)

Preheat the oven to 350 degrees. Lightly oil 12 muffin tin cups.

Place the cornmeal, flour, and baking powder in a large mixing bowl and mix well. In a separate bowl, combine the honey, egg, eggshell, if desired, yogurt, oil, and creamed corn and/or hot dog, if using. Add the wet mixture to the flour and stir until just blended.

Spoon the batter into the prepared cups and bake just until it is golden brown, 20 to 25 minutes. Set aside to cool to room temperature. Cover and refrigerate up to 3 days.

YIELD: 12 BISCUITS

SERVING SIZE: 1 BISCUIT (TOO MANY WILL SPOIL DINNER)

> We love to eat yogurt right out of the cup but also love to use it in cooking. It's a great way to sneak in an ingredient that assists digestion, improves intestinal function, and fortifies the body's natural defenses against a number of illnesses.

RACHEL TRAVERS'S DOGGIE BISCUITS TREAT

Boston food writer Rachel Travers does have the magic touch when it comes to dogs. These biscuits are based on a recipe handed down from her mother Bernice, and they're great. They're easy to whip up, taste *so* good, and keep forever. In other words, they're perfect. She likes them best with large and small bone-shaped cookie cutters.

1 cup unbleached all-purpose flour, plus extra for rolling

Vegetable oil

1 cup whole-wheat flour

½ cup wheat germ

½ cup nonfat dry milk

½ teaspoon salt

6 tablespoons margarine

1 large egg

1 teaspoon brown sugar

½ cup water

Preheat the oven to 325 degrees. Sprinkle a work surface with flour. Lightly grease a baking sheet.

Place the flours, wheat germ, dry milk, and salt in a bowl and mix to combine. Using two knives or a fork, cut in the margarine. Add the egg, sugar, and water and mix until well combined. Knead a few minutes. Place on floured surface and roll out ½ inch thick. Cut into shapes and place on the baking sheet. Bake 25 to 30 minutes. Turn off oven, leave until hard. Store in an airtight container.

YIELD: 24 LARGE BONES; 48 SMALL BONES

SERVING SIZE: 1 TO 2, DEPENDING ON THE SIZE OF THE BISCUIT

carrot doggo cake TREAT

Baby carrots are my all-time favorite vegetables, so I knew that carrot cake would be my kind of dessert. This is one of those miracle dishes that are absolutely scrumptious but also healthy. The carrots are, of course, full of vitamins; the peanuts and soy flour give you plenty of protein; the bananas are bursting with potassium. The chopped liver bits make it everything a dog could dream of.

FOR THE CAKE:

1 cup whole-wheat flour, plus additional for flouring the pan

1 teaspoon soy flour

1 teaspoon baking soda

¼ cup chopped unsalted peanuts

1 large egg

¼ cup vegetable oil, plus additional to grease the pan

1 tablespoon vanilla extract

⅓ cup honey

1 cup grated or ground carrots

Preheat the oven to 325 degrees. Lightly grease and flour an 8 x 12-inch baking pan.

To make the cake:
Place the whole-wheat and soy flour, baking soda, and chopped peanuts in a large bowl and mix to combine. Add the egg, oil, vanilla, honey, and carrots and mix until well combined. Pour the mixture into the prepared pan and bake until a toothpick comes out clean, 15 to 20 minutes. Set aside to cool on a wire rack.

> Don't be tempted to add raisins to this cake. They are potentially toxic to dogs.

FOR THE FROSTING:

2 cups mashed banana

1 tablespoon unsalted butter, at
room temperature

6 tablespoons carob powder

2 teaspoons vanilla extract

3 tablespoons unbleached all-
purpose flour

1 teaspoon ground cinnamon

Cooked chopped liver bits, for
garnish

To make the frosting:

Place all the ingredients in a mixer and mix until well
combined. Spread on the cooled cake. Cut into 18 pieces.
Garnish with chopped liver bits.
Cover and refrigerate up to
5 days.

YIELD: 18 PIECES

SERVING SIZE: 1 TO 2 PIECES

Also called St. John's bread (because John the Baptist is thought
to have eaten it) and locust bean,
carob is a great non-chocolate substitute for cocoa powder. High in B
vitamins, vitamin A, and minerals,
carob is twice as sweet as chocolate but has one third the calories
and is virtually fat and caffeine-
free.

Heaven goes by favor. If it went by merit, you would stay out and your dog would go in.
—Mark Twain

DEVIL DOG CAROB BROWNIES TREAT

Dogs can't have chocolate—and that's a tragedy, because dogs *like* chocolate very, very much. The problem is the caffeine in chocolate, or so humans tell us (do I smell a conspiracy? Just asking . . .). The great news is that carob, which tastes almost as good, doesn't have caffeine, so it's safe for canines. Admittedly, carob isn't quite Ghirardelli or Godiva, but it does have that warm chocolatey flavor that makes all living things happy. Cut these up into tiny squares and you can use them to induce all sorts of obedience and good behavior.

Vegetable oil
½ cup vegetable shortening
3 tablespoons honey
4 large eggs
4 eggshells, ground
1 teaspoon vanilla extract
1 cup whole-wheat flour
¼ cup carob powder
½ teaspoon baking powder
½ chopped nuts

Preheat the oven to 350 degrees. Lightly grease a 9 x 13-inch pan. Mix the shortening and honey in a large bowl with a fork until creamy. Add the remaining ingredients and mix until well combined. Pour into the prepared pan and bake for 25 minutes. Set aside to cool. Cut into 24 pieces. Brownies may be individually wrapped and frozen for up to 2 months.

YIELD: 24 PIECES

SERVING SIZE: 1 TO 2 PIECES

Do not let your dog eat chocolate of any kind. Dogs are sensitive to methylxanthines, which are found in both caffeine and theobromine, a key component of chocolate. Dogs cannot metabolize and excrete methylxanthines as efficiently as humans. The chocolate in milk chocolate is quite diluted, which is why many dogs can eat the occasional piece and not seem to experience toxic effects. This is not true of unsweetened chocolate, and since dogs are not as sensitive to the bitter taste as humans are, they may eat more of the concentrated, more toxic baker's chocolate if they get a chance.

Symptoms include vomiting, hyperactivity, restlessness, hypersensitivity to touch (a dog will jump when touched), and a very rapid heartbeat and breathing rate. A loss of control of leg muscles, muscle tremor seizures, general weakness, coma, and finally death can follow.

BOW-WOW BIRTHDay Cake TREAT

I was born on April 12, so anyone who wants to celebrate (that means *you*) should feel free to send gifts, flowers, bones, toys, and, most important, bake me a cake. I love cake! (By the way, I also love pie; last Thanksgiving I made off with half a pumpkin pie while Susan took her parents to see *Cabaret*. God, it was *great*. The pie, I mean, not the play—although I hear the play is pretty good too. But that's another story.) This is a particularly toothsome recipe, and it's all vegan, in case your dog—(or you)—observes a vegetarian diet. (I do love my meat, but this cake is so good that it doesn't need a bacon chaser to please me.)

For you *and* your dog! It's really good!

3½ cups whole-wheat or unbleached all-purpose flour

1 cup carob powder

½ cup arrowroot

2 teaspoons baking powder

1 teaspoon ground cinnamon

2½ cups maple syrup

2 cups soy milk

2 tablespoons apple cider vinegar

2½ cups canola oil

Preheat the oven to 350 degrees. Line a sheet pan with parchment paper.

Place the flour, carob, arrowroot, baking powder, and cinnamon in a large bowl and mix to combine.

Place the maple syrup, soy milk, vinegar, and oil and a large bowl and whisk until combined.

Add the maple syrup mixture to the flour mixture and mix well until combined. Pour the batter into the prepared pan and bake until a toothpick comes out clean, about 25 minutes. Set aside until cool. Cut into 24 squares. Cover and refrigerate up to 5 days or freeze up to one month.

YIELD: 24 SQUARES

SERVING SIZE: 1 SQUARE

cinnamon bites   TREAT

I developed a taste for cinnamon when I stole a piece of cinnamon toast during brunch one Sunday morning. I didn't really expect to like it (I was doing *research*!) but the warm, slightly spicy flavor tickled me, and I've been a devotee ever since. These little cookies are a good training treat because they smell so good; that helps me keep my mind on my job.

Vegetable oil

2 cups whole-wheat flour

½ cup soy flour

1 teaspoon ground cinnamon

1 cup skim milk

1 tablespoon honey

1 tablespoon vegetable oil, plus additional to grease the cookie sheet

1 cup shredded carrots or apple

Preheat the oven to 400 degrees. Lightly grease a cookie sheet. Place the flours and cinnamon in a bowl and mix well. Add the milk, honey, oil, and carrots and mix again. Using a cookie scoop, place 24 scoops of dough on the prepared sheet and bake for 30 minutes. Set aside to cool. Repeat with remaining dough. Store in airtight container for up to 2 weeks.

YIELD: 24 COOKIES

SERVING SIZE: 1 TO 2 COOKIES

peanut butter cookies

If you are looking for a great treat that lasts for ages, try these peanut butter biscuits. They're also a snap to make. With the extra nuts tossed in, they have tons of protein (but they do add extra calories, in case you're watching your hound's weight).

Vegetable oil

1 cup unbleached all-purpose flour, plus extra for rolling

1 cup natural peanut butter (no salt, no sugar, no preservatives)

1 cup skim milk

½ cup chopped peanuts, walnuts or pecans (optional)

1 cup whole-wheat flour

1 tablespoon baking powder

Preheat the oven to 375 degrees. Lightly grease a cookie sheet.

Place the peanut butter and milk in a food processor fitted with a steel blade and blend until smooth. Add the nuts, if using. Add the flours and baking powder and process until it forms a ball.

Place the dough on a lightly floured surface and knead until smooth. Roll out into ¼-inch thickness and cut with a bone-shaped cookie cutter or scoop tablespoon-size balls onto the sheet and flatten with your palm. Place 2 inches apart on the prepared cookie sheets. Bake until lightly browned, about 20 minutes. Set aside to cool.

Store in an airtight container in the refrigerator up to 3 weeks. Bring to room temperature before serving.

YIELD: APPROXIMATELY 36–48 COOKIES

SERVING SIZE: 1 TO 2 COOKIES

Also called monkeynuts or ground nuts, peanuts, considered perhaps the most ubiquitous nut, are not actually nuts at all. Peanuts are legumes (plants with seed pods that split along both sides) that grow underground.

MAIDA HEATTER'S BONE APPETIT ⬤ TREAT

Sweet biscuits are terrific (they are cookbook writer and dessert maven Maida Heatter's claim to fame), but sometimes a savory treat is just what I'm craving. These can be chicken-, beef-, or vegetable-flavored, and are marvelous no matter what. They take longer than the average biscuit to bake, but that's what makes them so wonderfully crunchy. They taste better than chewing a stick (a high compliment, in my opinion) and are probably better for your digestion. The powdered milk, yeast, and bonemeal make this a nicely balanced biscuit as well as a tasty one. If I have any extras I bring them for my friends in Mutt and Jeff's Doggy Daycare Dog Bus, which I ride almost every afternoon.

¼ cup unprocessed bran

1 cup whole-wheat flour

¼ cup raw wheat germ

1 tablespoon powdered bonemeal

1 tablespoon nutritional yeast

¼ cup nonfat dry milk

2 egg whites

1 (6 ounce) jar (about ⅔ cup) chicken, beef, or vegetable baby food

Preheat the oven to 300 degrees.

Place all the ingredients in a mixing bowl and stir well to combine. Form the dough into a mound and roll out onto a pastry cloth with a rolling pin until ⅓ inch thick. Cut into 12 to 18 cookies with cookie cutters. Place cookies on the baking sheet. Bake for one hour, turning them over halfway and reversing front to back. Turn the oven off and let cool 30 minutes. Remove from oven and let stand to cool. Store in an airtight container up to 2 weeks.

YIELD: 12 TO 18 PIECES

SERVING SIZE: 1 TO 2 PIECES

We love wheat germ (the heart of the wheat kernel) for its nutty flavor and crunchy texture. If that's not enough, it's also jam packed with protein, vitamin E, folic acid, phosphorous, thiamin, zinc, and magnesium. Be sure to store it in the refrigerator to avoid spoilage.

Smoothie

Back when I was in college, I lived on smoothies—oops! I think I'm channeling Sally. (The real truth is that when *I* was in college, I lived on kibble and beer.) Anyway, I've become a big fan of this creamy treat—good for my potassium and calcium needs, and really fun to slurp, especially in the summer.

4 cups plain yogurt

1 overripe banana

½ to 1 cup blueberries, strawberries, or raspberries

3 tablespoons natural peanut butter (no salt, no sugar, no preservatives)

1 teaspoon vanilla extract

Place all the ingredients in the bowl of a food processor fitted with a steel blade and process until smooth. Pour into ice cube trays and place in the freezer until solid, about one hour. Serve frozen.

YIELD: ABOUT 6 CUPS, 24 CUBES

SERVING SIZE: 2 TO 3 CUBES

> Bananas, like squash, mangoes, and tomato paste, are very high in potassium, which helps control blood pressure and may help maintain normal heart and artery function.

No one appreciates the very special genius of your conversation as the dog does.

—Christopher Morley

Puppy Power TREAT

I just love happy endings, so here's one of the happiest endings I know: in 1994, Christa and Chris Linzey worked at Camden Yards in Baltimore. When they left work after a day game, they noticed a young dog roaming around, apparently lost and alone. (That's the sad part. Now comes the happy part.) They adopted the pup, named him Camden, and gave him a nice new life. Camden, who's pictured here, had some health problems (sad part again), but Christa and Chris were undaunted and began feeding him natural kibble, fruit, and vegetables, and he thrived. What's more, they decided that Camden should enjoy many, many treats (good philosophy!). They decided they would make the treats themselves (since Chris was a professional chef), so they would be sure the treats were top-notch. Camden urged them on to greater and greater treat achievement (go, Camden!). Eventually Christa and Chris started 3C Baking Company so they could produce treats for all the dogs of the world. Their treats are made from all-natural human-quality ingredients without any added sugar, salt, eggs, or dairy; they're low-fat for the tubbies among us; have lots of fiber (good for the belly); and taste as great as they smell! They have Camden's bark of approval, too. And to think a little parking-lot pup started this whole thing.

These bars will become hard and crunchy. For a fun twist, you can drizzle melted carob chips over them.

½ cup rolled oats

2 cups whole-wheat flour

½ cup unsweetened applesauce

1 tablespoon ground cinnamon

1 tablespoon honey

½ cup water

Preheat the oven to 350 degrees.

Place the oats in the bowl of a food processor fitted with a steel blade. Pulse until it forms a rough powder, about 30 seconds.

Transfer the oats to the bowl of a mixer fitted with a paddle attachment. Add the flour, applesauce, cinnamon, and honey, and mix for about 30 seconds at low speed. Then, while the mixer is going, slowly add the water. When all the water has been added, turn off the mixer and scrape down the sides. Raise the speed to medium and mix until all ingredients are just incorporated and form a ball, 20 to 30 seconds.

Roll out the dough to approximately ⅛-inch, and cut into shapes with any cookie cutter. A dog bone-shaped cutter is recommended, but use your imagination! You can use hearts, cats, or even an apple-shaped cutter! (Be sure to re-roll and use any scraps.) Place the shapes on a nonstick baking sheet or a regular baking sheet lined with parchment paper, and bake until slightly golden, about 30 minutes. Set aside to cool. Store in an airtight container up to 2 weeks.

YIELD: ABOUT 60 TO 75

cooper's favorite websites

FOR PICTURES OF ME (AND OTHER GOOD-LOOKING DOGS)

www.oldyellersrevenge.com (Cami Johnson's website)

FOR INFORMATION ON HOW TO BE A NICE, WELL-BEHAVED DOG

www.whoswalkingwhodogtraining.com (Stacy Alldredge's website)
www.abetterpet.com (Rachel Friedman's website)

FOR GREAT TOYS, BEAUTIFUL BEDS, NICE LEASHES, AND OTHER GOODIES

www.dogtoys.com
www.doggiebliss.com
www.fetchpets.com
www.georgesf.com
www.gooddogexpress.com
www.lucythewonderdog.com
www.Sitstay.com

FOR GOOD THINGS TO CHEW

www.bullysticks.com
www.blackdogbakery.com
www.merrickpetdeli.com

FOR THINGS TO READ

www.ahvma.org (the website of the American holistic veterinary medical association)
www.saveadog.org
www.traveldog.com
www.urbandogmagazine.com
www.whole-dog-journal.com

COOPER'S BOOK LIST

CHILDREN'S AND YOUNG ADULT BOOKS

The Adventures of Taxi Dog by Debra and Sal Barracca

Arthur's New Puppy by Marc Brown

Basic Dog Training by Miller Watson

Because of Winn-Dixie by Kate Dicamillo

Call of the Wild / Klondike and Other Stories / The Sea-Wolf / White Fang
    by Jack London

Dogs by Amanda O'Neill

Dogs by David Taylor

Dogs: 47 Favorite Breeds, Appearance, History, Personality and Lore
    by Steven M. L. Aronson

Dog Tricks by Captain Arthur J. Haggerty and Carol Lea Benjamin

Go, Dog, Go! by Philip D. Eastman

Harry the Dirty Dog / No Roses for Harry by Gene Zion

Henry and Mudge series by Cynthia Rylant

Higglety Pigglety Pop!: Or There Must Be More to Life by Maurice Sendak

How to Talk to Your Dog by Jean Craighead George

Lad: A Dog by Albert Payson Terhune

Martha Speaks by Susan Meddaugh

Max Makes a Million by Maira Kalman

The Night I Followed the Dog by Nina Laden

Oh, Tucker! by Steven Kroll

Old Yeller by Fred Gipson

Open Me . . . I'm a Dog by Art Spiegelman

Puppy: A Practical Guide to Caring for Your Puppy ASPCA Pet Care Guides for Kids
    by Mark Evans; foreword by Roger Caras, ASPCA president

The Puppy Who Wanted a Boy by Jane Thayer

Santa Paws to the Rescue by Nicholas Edwards

Stay!: Keeper's Story by Lois Lowry

Strider by Beverly Cleary

Three Stories You Can Read to Your Dog by Sara Swan Miller

Walter the Farting Dog by William Kotzwinkle and Glenn Murray

Where the Red Fern Grows by Wilson Rawls

Whistle for Willie by Ezra Jack Keats

ADULT BOOKS

All Creatures Great and Small by James Herriot

Bark If You Love Me: A Woman-Meets-Dog Story by Louise Bernikow

Chicken Soup for the Cat and Dog Lover's Soul—Celebrating Pets as Family with Stories About Cats, Dogs and Other Critters, edited by Jack Canfield

Clara the Early Years: The Story of the Pug Who Ruled My Life by Margo Kaufman

A Dog's Life by Peter Mayle

My Dog Tulip by J. R. Ackerley

Pack of Two: The Intricate Bond Between People and Dogs by Caroline Knapp

Tails from the Bark Side: True Stories from the Family Dog Files by Brian Kilcommens and Sarah Wilson

COOPEr's MOVIE LIST FOr KIDS OF aLL aGes

The Adventures of Milo & Otis (G)

Air Bud Series

Beethoven (PG)

Beethoven's 2nd (PG)

Beethoven's 3rd (G)

Beethoven's 4th (G)

Cats and Dogs (PG)

Dr. Dolittle (PG-13)

Dr. Dolittle 2 (PG)

Homeward Bound—The Incredible Journey (G)

Homeward Bound II—Lost in San Francisco (G)

Lassie Come Home

My Dog Skip (PG)

Old Yeller (G)

Shaggy DA

Shaggy Dog

TABLE OF EQUIVALENTS

LIQUID AND DRY MEASURES

U.S.	METRIC
¼ teaspoon	1.25 milliliters
½ teaspoon	2.5 milliliters
1 teaspoon	5 milliliters
1 tablespoon (3 teaspoons)	15 milliliters
1 fluid ounce (2 tablespoons)	30 milliliters
¼ cup	65 milliliters
⅓ cup	80 milliliters
1 cup	235 milliliters
1 pint (2 cups)	480 milliliters
1 quart (4 cups, 32 ounces)	950 milliliters
1 gallon (4 quarts)	3.8 liters
1 ounce (by weight)	28 grams
1 pound	454 grams
2.2 pounds	1 kilogram

LENGTH MEASURES

U.S.	METRIC
⅛ inch	3 millimeters
¼ inch	6 millimeters
½ inch	12 millimeters
1 inch	2.5 centimeters

OVEN TEMPERATURES

FAHRENHEIT	CELSIUS	GAS
250	120	½
275	140	1
300	150	2
325	160	3
350	180	4
375	190	5
400	200	6
425	220	7
450	230	8
475	240	9
500	260	10

*The exact equivalents in the above tables have been rounded off for convenience.

index

ABOUT THE AUTHORS

Cooper Gillespie is a Welsh springer spaniel. He enjoys swimming and eating plastic and chicken. He lives with Susan Orlean, the bestselling author of *The Orchid Thief,* which was made into the movie *Adaptation*.

Sally Sampson is the author and coauthor of ten cookbooks, including *Souped Up!* and the James Beard Award–nominated *The $50 Dinner Party*.

Photographer Cami Johnson specializes in animal portraits. She lives in Boston with her two dogs, Max and Sunny, and a cat named Kibbles. Her website is www.oldyellersrevenge.com.